PRAISE

The Holy Spirit is our greatest resource for accomplishing the Great Commission, the very purpose for which Jesus has left his bride, the church, on earth. Prayer is the way we access that resource so, to fulfill our purpose, followers of Jesus must know how to pray! Thankfully, Jesus teaches us how through His model prayer. In his book on prayer, Pastor GJ Farmer offers wonderful insights to the reader concerning the deep and symbolic meaning of our Lord's Prayer. As you read it, I trust that you, like me, will be both challenged and encouraged in your prayer life.

Paul Chitwood
President, International Mission Board of the Southern Baptist Convention

We see it all the time. The Lord's prayer is repeated ritualistically and routinely before an event. Then the participants proceed to go and act in ways distinctly different from what they just "prayed." Even as believers, there are many times that rituals and routines can unintentionally take over in our lives. GJ Farmer's book, *Teach Us to Pray*, is an excellent resource to help any believer refocus on what it truly means to pray to our heavenly Father in the way He desires for us to pray and draw closer to Him. You will enjoy the practical illustrations and applications GJ provides that will help you to discover God's heart in the way our Lord intended His model prayer to be used.

Donnie Fox
President, Clear Creek Baptist Bible College

GJ Farmer, in his interaction with Matthew 6, answers the question, "How should we pray?" He does an excellent job of breaking it down and making it simple while remaining faithful to the text. People who read this book, whether new in the faith or a mature believer, will find themselves wanting to stop reading and start praying. I highly recommend *Teach Us to Pray*.

Todd Gray

Executive Director-Treasurer, Kentucky Baptist Convention

TEACH US TO PRAY

DISCOVERING GOD'S HEART THROUGH JESUS'S MODEL PRAYER

GJ FARMER

DEDICATION

To my Lord, Jesus Christ.
For His eternal and undeserved grace, mercy, and
favor in my life.

To my wife, Hillary.
For her unconditional love and daily sacrifices for our
children and me.

CONTENTS

– INTRODUCTION –

Do you remember a recent time you learned something new? For me, it was when I went tent camping with some of my friends. I'm not an outdoorsman, but they talked me into going, and I knew I was in for a steep learning curve. To prepare, I watched Bear Grylls the night before (as if that were going to do something) and went with the adage my dad used to say, "Fake it 'till you make it." Even still, I had much to learn in that experience. From taking fish off the line to figuring out how to choose the right spot to set up your tent, I tended to rely on the skills of others who were with me.

Similarly, those of us who pray had to learn how to do so at some point in our lives. You may have learned from watching your parents pray as you were a child, or perhaps a family member or Sunday School teacher taught you the basics of what to say and do.

In Matthew 6, we find Jesus preaching what is known as the Sermon on the Mount. If you have never read the entirety of this sermon, in Matthew 5-7, I highly encourage you to do so. Within His message, Jesus devotes some of His content to teaching His hearers how to pray. We are going to spend the majority of this book, analyzing how Jesus taught them to pray and how we are to apply this prayer to our lives. But first, let's take a look at the reason Jesus thought it necessary to teach how to pray.

As we observe Jesus's audience for this sermon, we find a large group of people, presumably mostly Jews, along with Jesus's disciples (Matt. 5:1). These people were not unfamiliar with praying. The Jews were raised around the teachings of the law and the prophets of the Old Testament. They knew how to pray and had been praying since childhood. However, for some, prayer had become a ritual. It had become routine and a way to impress others.

In the first four verses of Matthew 6, Jesus addresses the issue of hypocrisy in giving to the poor.

Be careful not to practice your righteousness in front of others to be seen by them. Otherwise, you have no reward with your Father in heaven. So whenever you give to the poor, don't sound a trumpet before you, as the hypocrites do in the synagogues and on the streets, to be applauded by people. Truly I tell you, they have their reward. But when you give to the poor, don't let your left hand know what your right hand is doing, so that your giving may be in secret. And your Father who sees in secret will reward you.
(Matthew 6:1-4)

Next, Jesus exposes the insincerity that had crept into the people's prayers, continuing His theme of addressing hypocritical behavior.

Whenever you pray, you must not be like the hypocrites, because they love to pray standing in the synagogues and on the street corners to be seen by people. Truly I tell you, they have their reward. But when you pray, go into your private room, shut your door, and pray to your Father who is in secret. And your Father who sees in secret will reward you. When you pray, don't babble like the Gentiles, since they imagine they'll be heard for their many words. Don't be like them, because your Father knows the things you need before you ask him.
(Matthew 6:5-8)

The primary reason Jesus gave them this model prayer was not because they weren't praying with their lips, but that they weren't genuine in their hearts. They were seeking the praise of men rather than the praise of God. They were hypocrites with their prayers.

God calls us to inspect our hearts in the same way Jesus challenged the people to check theirs: Why do you pray? Are you trying to impose your will on God? Are you trying to impress Him or others with your many words or very public prayers?

God knows your inner thoughts and your most significant needs. There is nothing that you are going to petition to Him that will surprise Him. There is also no way that you can pray that will make Him love you any more or less than He already does. His love is perfect and never fails.

When you go to God, go to Him in confidence, knowing He cares more about you and your needs than even you do. In your praying, He sees your heart. There's no requirement for impressive language or for lengthy prayers (if you've been nervous about praying in public because you thought you couldn't do this well, you should find this freeing). Simply bear your soul to Him, knowing and clinging to His love for and

4

faithfulness to you.

Since you're reading a book on prayer, I likely don't have to convince you of the necessity of it or the fact that God hears and answers prayer. Instead, we are going to focus the remainder of this book on what Jesus taught in Matthew 6, answering the question, "How should we pray?"

As we seek to discover the answer to this question, I think you too will notice from this prayer what I have come to find—this model isn't so much to teach us how to bring our requests to God as it is about moving us to wrap our hearts, minds, and wills around God's. And if we're honest, we all have room to grow in those areas.

Lord, teach us to pray.

Therefore, you should pray like this: Our Father in heaven, your name be honored as holy.
Your kingdom come. Your will be done on earth as it is in heaven.
Give us today our daily bread.
And forgive us our debts, as we also have forgiven our debtors.
And do not bring us into temptation, but deliver us from the evil one.
(Matthew 6:9-13)

– OUR FATHER IN HEAVEN –

Therefore, you should pray like this: Our Father in heaven, your name be honored as holy. Your kingdom come. Your will be done on earth as it is in heaven...
(Matthew 6:9-10)

It likely wasn't the statement, "You should pray like this," that most captured the attention of Jesus's audience when He was teaching on prayer. Instead, when He revealed their ability to know and pray to God as their Father, it was revolutionary.

The nation of Israel had always viewed God as an all-powerful, supreme authority (which He is), and because of this, they felt they must come before Him with fear and trembling. Jesus opened the door for believers to go to God, not just as Sovereign of the universe, but as Father. The New Testament letter to the Hebrews expounds on what this means.

> **JESUS OPENED THE DOOR FOR US TO COME TO GOD NOT JUST AS THE SOVEREIGN OF THE UNIVERSE, BUT AS FATHER.**

Therefore, let us approach the throne of grace with boldness, so that we may receive mercy and find grace to help us in time of need.
(Hebrews 4:16)

Because we can know God in this way, we can approach His throne in confidence, without fear.

"Father" in Greek captures the Aramaic sense of "Abba," which in English, we would say, "Daddy." Imagine the countenance on people's faces when they heard for the first time that they could come to God as their Daddy. When you have a relationship with God, through Jesus, you too can know God in this close, personal way (for more information on how to have a relationship with God, be sure to read Appendix 3).

WE SHOULD DESIRE FOR GOD'S NAME TO BE REVERED.

Stop for a moment and consider what's in a name. My first name, Gregory, means "watchman." I would like to think I emulate this characteristic in my life, but candidly, I wasn't named Gregory because of my watch-care abilities. I was named after my dad.

In today's American culture, some children are given their names because of the meaning behind them. However, I would venture to say that most of us choose our children's names because of the sound or sentimental meaning of them. Either way, the ritual of naming a child has developed into a much different practice today than in ancient times.

In Jesus's day, there was great significance behind the choice of a name. A baby's name might express something his parents had learned through his arrival or a character quality they envisioned for his life (i.e., Isaac, Gen. 21:3-7). Additionally, Scripture records multiple times that someone's name was changed when something about their character changed (i.e., Jacob to Israel, Gen. 32:28; Simon to Peter, John 1:42).

Marking the prayer's first petition to God, Jesus prays for our Father's name to be honored as holy.

God's name is the name that is above all names. It is the name that holds the most incredible power, authority, and is holy, holy,

holy. He doesn't need us to pray for His name to be honored as holy for it to be so. This fact then begs the question, "If God's name already is holy, why are we praying for His name to be honored as holy?"

Remember, this prayer is not for God's benefit, but ours. This statement is for us to lay our hearts before the Lord's throne and pray, "In my life, may your name be honored as holy."

Yes, we can know God as closely as a Father, but in knowing Him in this personal way, there is a balance that we must strike between closeness and reverence. While it was shocking for the Jews to think of God as a Father, I'm afraid some two-thousand years later that the pendulum may have swung the other direction entirely.

> **HAVE YOU BECOME SO COMFORTABLE WITH GOD AS YOUR FATHER THAT YOU'VE FORGOTTEN HE'S ALSO YOUR KING?**

Let me pose this question to you—have you become so comfortable with God being your Father that you've forgotten He's also your King? In other words, have you lost your reverence for God?

Do you honor God's name as holy? Do you treat it as the name above all names, or do you speak of Him, using the term God, Jesus, or Lord, casually or even as slang or a curse word? Is how you live, bearing the name of Christ, bringing honor or shame to Him? Our desire to honor God's name must be more than a prayer; our lifestyles must embrace it. May our words and deeds continually display our prayerful desire, "Father, let Your name be honored as holy in my life."

WE SHOULD DESIRE FOR GOD'S KINGDOM TO COME.

The Christmas season brings much joy in my life. Growing up, I loved the anticipation and excitement surrounding all the events. Now my enjoyment for Christmas is found in seeing that eagerness exhibited in my children.

Many people countdown the days until Christmas arrives. We mark off our calendars and watch for the signs of its coming. One of the first noticeable signs that the holiday is approaching is when ornaments, bows, and wrapping paper are lining the shelves at your local Hobby Lobby. It's at that moment you know, Christmas is only about nine months away.

Months later, the temperature begins to change, you hear Christmas music on the radio, and see lights on houses. Those signs genuinely let you know that Christmas is nearing!

In the same way, there are signs we are to watch in anticipation of God's kingdom's coming. In a sense, God's kingdom has already arrived (eternal life as a present reality for believers, the indwelling of the Holy Spirit, etc.), but we should long for its full realization to come to pass. This yearning is why Jesus said we should pray, "Your kingdom come."

Revelation 21 gives us a picture of what this day will look like:

Then I saw a new heaven and a new earth; for the first heaven and the first earth had passed away, and the sea was no more. I also saw the holy city, the new Jerusalem, coming down out of heaven from God, prepared like a bride adorned for her husband. Then I heard a loud voice from the throne: Look, God's dwelling is with humanity, and he will live with them. They will be his peoples, and God himself will be with them and will be their God. He will wipe away every tear from their eyes. Death will be no more; grief, crying, and pain will be no more, because the previous things have passed away.
(Revelation 21:1-4)

A Christian response to this passage should be eagerness building within the heart.

I wonder if we sometimes like the idea of God's kingdom coming in theory, but not in practice. As we perceive what could be apocalyptic situations playing out in our world through politics and government, it seems as if the words of Jesus in Matthew 24 could be coming true today.

Instead of excitement for Jesus's arrival, however, I have seen many Christians post news articles and opinion pieces on social media, which seem laced with fear. Their headlines include ideas of potential prophecies coming to pass—"one-world government," "cashless society," and "mark of the beast."

While much of this connection with biblical prophecy is speculation at this point, the principle remains—if certain events must happen to usher in the kingdom of God, should we not long for them to take place? Instead of, "God forbid," should we not exclaim, "Bring it on!"? There should be no fear in the heart of the Christian. Why should we worry since we will be kept in the hand of the Lord?

> THERE SHOULD BE NO FEAR IN THE HEART OF THE CHRISTIAN. WHY SHOULD WE WORRY SINCE WE ARE KEPT IN THE HAND OF THE LORD?

In praying, "Your kingdom come," we

are reciprocating the shout of the apostle John:

He who testifies about these things says, "Yes,
I am coming soon." Amen! Come, Lord Jesus!
(Revelation 22:20)

WE SHOULD DESIRE FOR GOD'S WILL TO BE DONE.

It isn't uncommon for us to pray for God's will to be done. Usually, we do so in a situation where we aren't sure what God's best for us entails. For example, when my dad found out he had stage four cancer several years ago, everyone was praying for his total healing. But we were also praying for God's will to be done. We prayed this knowing if God had something different and better in mind, that is what we should long for because God's will is always superior to ours.

In praying for God's will for our lives, we are, in essence, declaring that God has total control, and we fully submit to Him.

That can be scary if we don't fully trust Him. And honestly, we aren't always good at submitting. Total submission is completely giving over our will to God's.

This idea of submission reminds me of how I felt when I recently took my oldest son to the Corvette Museum in Bowling Green, Kentucky. He is seven years old and enjoys looking at cars and driving them on video games. The museum had a simulator that allowed you to sit inside a real Corvette body and steer as it turned and rumbled with the images on the screens. Of course, I had to let my son give it a go. What young boy wouldn't want to have an opportunity to drive his dad, especially in a Corvette?

It felt strange to submit myself to his driving and ride in the passenger seat, even if it was a simulation. I can only imagine how frightening it would be if it were a reality.

While it is understandable to be nervous about submitting your life to a child, there is absolutely nothing we should worry about when we surrender our lives to the will of God. His way may not always be easy, but it will always be best.

To pray for God's will to be done in your life as it is in heaven means that you want His will to be accomplished entirely in and through you, no matter the cost.

You may ask, how can I do God's will if I don't know what it is? Good question. We spend much time on our knees asking God to show us His will when He's already revealed it to us in His Word. If you want to live out God's will, you must spend time daily in the Scriptures. You must ask God to mold you and conform you more into the image of His Son through your obedience to His Word. You will then be able to say that your sincere desire is for His will to be done in you as it is in heaven.

> **WE SPEND MUCH TIME ON OUR KNEES ASKING GOD TO SHOW US HIS WILL WHEN HE'S ALREADY REVEALED IT TO US IN HIS WORD.**

What would it look like if God's will was accomplished perfectly through you in your private life, in your family, in your workplace, in your witness for Christ? Through the power of the Holy Spirit, God calls us not to just pray for His will to be done, but to then pursue His holiness in our lives.

QUESTIONS FOR CONSIDERATION

1. How has your view of God as your Father changed as you have come to know Him more?

2. How do you need to honor God's name in a more significant way?

3. If Jesus were going to return tomorrow, how might that change how you live today? Would it bring you joy or anxiety?

4. Do you find it easy or difficult to submit to God's will? Why?

– GIVE US OUR DAILY BREAD –

Give us today our daily bread.
(Matthew 6:11)

Have you ever begun something that seemed extremely simple and soon became very complicated? I asked my friends this question on Facebook and received numerous replies such as parenting, marriage, learning a subject in school, and even retirement. By far, the most popular response surrounded the task of putting together some type of furniture (Amen to that!).

This feeling we have all experienced captures how I felt when studying this verse. On the surface, it appeared very straightforward and easy to understand. But the more I dug into this passage, the more complicated it became.

The most challenging portion of this verse is in translating the Greek term for "daily." In English, it doesn't appear to be too complicated. However, if you look at this verse in a Bible with footnotes, you'll likely discover that the translators have given specific attention to this word and have offered various ways to translate it. These other translations often span definitions such as "necessary bread," and "bread for tomorrow."

The reason for these variances is that linguists believe Matthew may have invented a Greek word to help his readers more accurately understand what Jesus was teaching that day (Jesus would have been speaking in Aramaic).[1] As a result, there is no one English word that can fully encompass what Jesus meant by, "Daily bread."

In this chapter, we are going to explore the meaning of this word in its full sense and consider three mindsets we are to have when praying, "Give us today our daily bread."

MINDSET #1: FATHER, I ACKNOWLEDGE THAT MY PROVISIONS COME FROM YOU ALONE.

By approaching God's throne with the words, "Give us," especially when speaking of something as essential as food, we are first acknowledging that He is our sole provider. To ask God for something is to recognize, He is capable of providing. In a sense, we are praying, "Father, I acknowledge that my provisions come from You alone."

> **TO ASK GOD FOR SOMETHING IS TO RECOGNIZE, HE IS CAPABLE OF PROVIDING.**

Conversely, many of us sometimes fall for the lie that we are our providers. Culture tells us we *work* hard for our money, we have *earned* everything we have, and we *deserve* it all. Jesus's hearers, many likely being farmers due to Israel's landscape, could have come to believe this too if they viewed themselves as disconnected from God. They *tilled* the land, *planted* the seeds, and *reaped* the harvest. Any of them could have said, "I work by the sweat of my brow. No one gave me this; I did this!"

These agrarians were likely the people Jesus spoke directly to just a few sentences later when He reassured them of God's provision for them if they sought Him first.

Consider the birds of the sky: They don't sow or reap or gather into barns, yet your heavenly Father feeds them. Aren't you worth more than they?
(Matthew 6:26)

When the temptation to believe you provide for yourself rises, reflect on the words of Psalm 89:11.

The heavens are Yours; the earth also is Yours.
The world and everything in it—You founded them.
(Psalm 89:11)

As a child, occasionally, I attempted to lay claim of my bedroom and declare that I was allowed to do what I wanted in MY room. The same occurrence would usually follow this misguided entitlement—me being set straight by my parents. It often seems that children don't learn and appreciate all their parents do for them until they mature and become adults themselves.

Like immature or unappreciative children, we can come to view our Heavenly Father's provision for us through a distorted lens.

God's Word never portrays man as being his own provider. How dare we say to our Creator, the One who owns it all, that we are our caretakers?! We, too, must mature, as children of God, recognizing from where our provisions come.

> **GOD'S WORD NEVER PORTRAYS MAN AS BEING HIS OWN PROVIDER.**

When you are tempted to have a misguided sense of pride, go to the Lord and confess it. May we be known as people who continually thank Him for being our provider in all areas of life.

MINDSET #2: FATHER, I TRUST YOU TO TAKE CARE OF ME.

When speaking to Americans of "the freedoms we have," you likely don't have to explain what that means. Americans grow up understanding that we have undeniable liberties in this country, paved by our ancestors in this nation's founding, and defended by those who serve in our military.

However, if you were reading about "the freedoms Americans had" through the eyes of a different culture, thousands of years later, you most certainly would have to do some research to comprehend the phrase's significance.

In the same way, there is a bit of cultural information that we must recognize to grasp the full understanding of Jesus's teaching on daily bread. Jesus taught on God's faithfulness, assuring His hearers that God would supply the needs of those who sought Him.

But seek first the kingdom of God and his righteousness, and all these things will be provided for you.
(Matthew 6:33)

This understanding of God's faithfulness and provision was believed and embraced throughout the whole Jewish community because they had learned this from their ancestors' experience. They passed the stories down from generation to generation.

The account of Israel receiving manna from God is a prime example. In Exodus 16, the Hebrews had been liberated from slavery in Egypt. God was leading them to the land that He had promised to them, but, because of their fear and disobedience, they found themselves wandering in the wilderness for forty years instead. During this time, the people were hungry and complained to God's appointed leaders, Moses and Aaron. God heard their grumblings and responded by sending bread from heaven (manna) each morning, as well as quail in the evenings.

But to make sure the Hebrews learned to trust His faithfulness, God had some specific instructions for how they were to collect and use this food.

The entire Israelite community grumbled against Moses and Aaron in the wilderness. The Israelites said to them, "If only we had died by the LORD's hand in the land of Egypt, when we sat by pots of meat and ate all the bread we wanted. Instead, you brought us into this wilderness to make this whole assembly die of hunger!"
Then the LORD said to Moses, "I am going to rain bread from heaven for you. The people are to go out each day and gather enough for that day. This way I will test them to see whether or not they will follow my instructions. On the sixth day, when they prepare what they bring in, it will be twice as much as they gather on other days."
(Exodus 16:2-5)

Notice when God explicitly told them to collect it—daily (other than on the sixth day, because He commanded them to rest on the Sabbath). He wanted them to realize that He would take care of them.

From their experiences of God's faithfulness in the past, the Jews continued teaching this truth to others, generations later. They had learned to pray daily and ask for God's provision because they trusted Him to take care of them.

While our situations will likely differ from the Israelites in the wilderness, the principle remains the same. God will provide those who seek His kingdom and righteousness first, with precisely what they need to accomplish His will in their lives. In modeling the prayer of, "Give us *today*," Jesus teaches us to pray, "Father, I trust You to take care of me."

If you ever begin to doubt God's faithfulness, consider what He has already done.

> IF YOU EVER BEGIN TO DOUBT GOD'S FAITHFULNESS, CONSIDER WHAT HE HAS ALREADY DONE.

In fact, why don't you do that now? Stop reading just for a moment and ponder a few ways God has shown Himself faithful to you in the past month and prayerfully declare your faith in Him today.

MINDSET #3: FATHER, I ASK YOU FOR JUST ENOUGH.

I'm writing this toward the end of summer in 2020. A lot has happened recently in the news, given the Coronavirus pandemic that has plagued the world. Many have searched for various forms of aid and relief through the pain and loss they have experienced. One way governments have assisted their citizens is by offering monetary relief through welfare programs. For many in this time, this relief is a real answer to prayer.

Various Christian news sources have reported on a Chinese Christian church member in her 80's, who had her welfare check delivered. Articles stated that when she received it from the government officials at her door, she exclaimed, "Thank God!" As a result, the officials informed her that she would be removed from the aid list because she praised God, rather than the Communist Party for the help she received.

Another Christian recounted a similar story of Chinese officials raiding his home and removing all Christian-related décor (crosses, photos of Jesus, etc.) and replacing them with Chinese government leaders' pictures. They demanded the Christians in the home worship the leaders instead of Jesus.[2]

Put yourself in the shoes of those believers for a moment. When our refrigerators are full of food, money is in our bank accounts, and we are free to worship at church on Sundays, it's easy to say we acknowledge our provisions come from God alone and believe He will take care of us. It becomes much more challenging to proclaim it amid trials and testing. Could you still assert this if you were living in modern-day China?

As if this challenge were not already monumental enough, Jesus takes the trust-factor up another notch by using this term, "daily" bread. Again, this Greek word is a complicated word to translate in English, with the options being between "daily," "necessary," and "bread for tomorrow." After research, I conclude that the best way to interpret this idea of "daily bread" is by blending each of these meanings into one thought.

Let me clarify how I arrived at this position. Remember, it all points back to Jesus's hearers' understanding of the story of manna and having faith in God's provision.

Let's look at the continuation of this story from Exodus 16:

So at evening quail came and covered the camp. In the morning there was a layer of dew all around the camp. When the layer of dew evaporated, there were fine flakes on the desert surface, as fine as frost on the ground. When the Israelites saw it, they asked one another, "What is it?" because they didn't know what it was.

Moses told them, "It is the bread the LORD has given you to eat. This is what the LORD has commanded: 'Gather as much of it as each person needs to eat. You may take two quarts per individual, according to the number of people each of you has in his tent.'"

So the Israelites did this. Some gathered a lot, some a little. When they measured it by quarts, the person who gathered a lot had no surplus, and the person who gathered a little had no shortage. Each gathered as much as he needed to eat. Moses said to them, "No one is to let any of it remain until morning." But they didn't listen to Moses; some people left part of it until morning, and it bred worms and stank. Therefore Moses was angry with them.
(Exodus 16:13-20)

In the wilderness, God instructed the Hebrews to collect the bread they needed each morning, only taking enough for themselves for that day. But instead of consuming all of what they had taken, they rationed it, making sure to save some for the next day just in case

God didn't come through. See the issue?

It's one thing to acknowledge that God is your provider and trust He will take care of you. It's another to believe these truths so strongly that if He commanded you to do so, you would be willing to leave nothing to spare for the next day.

This unhindered obedience is the level of trust God wants His people to have in Him. In times of plenty or in times of scarcity, when the government rips your only source of income away, we are called to pray with a spirit that declares, "Father, I trust You and ask only for just enough. Not for excess because I am unsure of tomorrow, but for whatever You deem as necessary for me." Proverbs 30:8 echoes the words of this type of prayer:

Keep falsehood and deceitful words far from me.
Give me neither poverty nor wealth;
feed me with the food I need.
(Proverbs 30:8)

Now let's go back to Matthew 6 and wrap this up. Notice what we have gleaned in this verse from Jesus's teaching:

- "Give us…" (Father, I acknowledge my provisions come from You alone.)

- "…today…" (Father, I trust You to take care of me.)
- "…our daily bread." (Father, I ask You for just enough.)

Praying for daily bread isn't essentially about asking God for food, as many have thought. According to His will, God has promised to meet the needs of those who seek Him. Praying for daily bread is about declaring our trust in God's provision and displaying our confidence in Him by asking for only what He deems as enough.

> **PRAYING FOR DAILY BREAD IS ABOUT DECLARING OUR TRUST IN GOD'S PROVISION AND DISPLAYING OUR CONFIDENCE IN HIM BY ASKING FOR ONLY WHAT HE DEEMS AS ENOUGH.**

Jesus knew we needed to pray about this daily because we tend to think more highly of ourselves than we should. This tendency is why Proverbs 30 goes on to say:

Keep falsehood and deceitful words far from me.
Give me neither poverty nor wealth;
feed me with the food I need.
Otherwise, I might have too much
and deny you, saying, "Who is the LORD?"

or I might have nothing and steal,
profaning the name of my God.
(Proverbs 30:8-9)

God's Word repeatedly warns of the dangers of wealth and the unlikely nature for rich people to enter the kingdom since we often are tempted to deny God and look to ourselves as our providers. On the other hand, if we believe we have too little, we tend to want more and to take it upon ourselves to fulfill our desires, perhaps even stooping to the level of sin to do so.

You can depend on God. His provisions may not arrive at your doorstep. He will likely require some effort from you as He does the birds, but He is faithful. What would it look like for you to trust Him fully? I'm confident you would be less worried. You likely would have more peace in your life. As a response to fully trusting God to provide for your needs, you could become more generous to others. Today, in prayer, embrace the words of the Psalmist:

Those who know your name trust in you
because you have not abandoned
those who seek you, LORD.
(Psalm 9:10)

QUESTIONS FOR CONSIDERATION

1. Are you taking any of God's provisions for granted? If so, what do you need to thank God for today?

2. On a scale of 1-10, how consistent is your "daily" prayer life? What might need to change to make it more consistent?

3. We are all called to give, especially if God has given you excess. What are some ways you can bless others and build the kingdom of God through your giving?

---

[1] See Anthony Harvey's article, "Daily Bread," in The Journal of Theological Studies, NS, Vol. 69, Pt. 1, April 2018.

[2] See the article, *"China orders Christians to renounce faith in Jesus & worship President Xi Jinping instead,"* at https://www.christiantoday.com/article/china-tells-christians-renounce-faith-in-jesus-worship-president-xi-jinping/135221.htm (Accessed Aug. 5, 2020).

– FORGIVE US OUR DEBTS –

And forgive us our debts,
as we also have forgiven our debtors.
(Matthew 6:12)

I truly believe one of the most significant lies our culture has bought into is that our sin hurts no one. Many think they can live in disregard for God with little to no consequences, so long as it does no apparent damage to themselves or others.

As you can tell from the title of this chapter and the key verse, we are going to spend some time savoring God's magnificent forgiveness. But let's first correct any flawed view of sin that we may have.

WITHOUT CHRIST, OUR SINS CAUSE INSURMOUNTABLE SPIRITUAL DEBT

If a group of people, who had memorized this model prayer, began reciting it, up until now, things would have likely been relatively uniform. It's at this verse that they would start to diverge, with some saying, "forgive us our debts," and others recounting the traditional, "forgive us our trespasses."

In Greek, the term we find Jesus using is literally "debt," as in something owed to someone else (I'll explain in a bit why traditionally we have heard the term "trespasses" instead).

The concept of debt carries with it a couple of different notions. In one sense, we can generate debt for something given to us on credit. This type of debt is likely the kind most of us are familiar with—mortgages, car payments, student loans, etc. Not a very good feeling, but at least you have something to show for it. In another sense, one assumes debt when he owes for a wrong that has been committed. Today, this could occur from a speeding ticket, restitution for a crime, or a court settlement.

Jesus's hearers would have been familiar with both of these types of debt. Farmers of that day would have commonly sold most of their crops for income while retaining some for their families. Still, there would occasionally be years of drought that would leave them having to take on debt, sometimes so much that they would have to work as slave labor to pay it off. If the debt became large enough, their wives and children would have to work as well.

The Bible teaches that we each owe a debt for our sins. That debt amounts to eternal death.

For the wages of sin is death...
(Romans 6:23a)

When we choose to sin, we are guilty of trespassing into a forbidden area and, as a result, stand guilty before God.

Again, many have bought into the lie that sin is no big deal. If questioned, it's likely most would say they are good people. You may have even thought that about yourself. I mean, after all, we haven't done anything THAT bad, have we? Candidly, we tend to measure ourselves against our

> **WE TEND TO MEASURE OURSELVES AGAINST OUR SUBJECTIVE STANDARD OF GOODNESS RATHER THAN THE OBJECTIVE STANDARD GOD HAS SET—HOLINESS.**

subjective standard of goodness rather than the objective standard God has set—holiness.

"...There is only one who is good..."
(Matthew 19:17)

For all have sinned and fall short of the glory of God;
(Romans 3:23)

Growing up, I remember an occasion where a vacuum cleaner salesman came to our home. This sort of thing used to be much more common than it is today. His sales pitch involved asking us to bring out our current vacuum and use it to clean an area of our choosing on our carpet. We then proceeded to vacuum until we were confident the space was clean.

Once we completed our part of the process, the salesman snapped together his vacuum and powered it on. After a few moments of cleaning the same area, he turned it off, revealing the grime our vacuum had left behind that his had picked up. It was apparent that our standard for clean carpets was much lower than his.

Our carpet was much filthier than we even imagined, and so it is with our lives. Against the backdrop of God's holiness, our shortcomings immediately become evident. Man's

> **AGAINST THE BACKDROP OF GOD'S HOLINESS, OUR SHORTCOMINGS IMMEDIATELY BECOME EVIDENT.**

standard for morality typically concerns itself solely with the outward appearances, while God's standard is first concerned with the heart. Jesus sought for His listeners to consider their hearts.

You have heard that it was said to our ancestors, Do not murder, and whoever murders will be subject to judgment. But I tell you, everyone who is angry with his brother or sister will be subject to judgment. Whoever insults his brother or sister, will be subject to the court. Whoever says, "You fool!" will be subject to hellfire.
(Matthew 5:21-22)

You have heard that it was said, Do not commit adultery. But I tell you, everyone who looks at a woman lustfully has already committed adultery with her in his heart.
(Matthew 5:27-28)

Enter through the narrow gate. For the gate is wide and the road broad that leads to destruction, and there are many who go through it. How narrow is the gate and difficult the road that leads to life, and few find it. (Matthew 7:13-14)

We all have fallen dramatically short of God's standard, but is eternal punishment in Hell a suitable punishment for these seemingly harmless acts of sin we've committed?

This example is often told to help reveal the seriousness of our sin: Suppose a child decided to lie to his friends. What sort of ramifications could he expect? His friends may become upset with him or stop talking to him for a while. Now, if that child also lied to his parents, he may then expect to be grounded or for them to give him some other form of punishment.

What if that child grew up, continued to lie, and told a falsehood to his boss? He may be scolded or fired. And if this individual lied to a police officer? A few months to a year in jail. Finally, if he became so bold in his habitual lying, he did so to Congress or the FBI? He would find himself receiving up to 5 years in prison.

What changed in each instance of this illustration? It wasn't the sin. It wasn't the guilty person. The only two factors that changed were who the individual sinned against and the penalty for the wrongdoing. The greater the authority the offended party had over the individual, the harsher the punishment.

Just before His ascension into heaven, Jesus proclaimed:

> *...All authority has been given to me in heaven and on earth.*
> *(Matthew 28:18b)*

No one has more authority over humanity than our Creator. Therefore, since every sin we commit is against Him, we are deserving of the most severe punishment possible.

Yet, there is good news.

GOD IS WILLING TO FORGIVE

The good news of the gospel is that God is willing to forgive your debts because of Jesus's death and resurrection. Jesus, being fully God and fully man, lived a sinless life yet took our

THE GOOD NEWS OF THE GOSPEL IS THAT GOD IS WILLING TO FORGIVE YOUR DEBTS BECAUSE OF JESUS'S DEATH AND RESURRECTION.

sin upon Himself when He died on the cross. For those who are in Christ, God's wrath has been satisfied through Jesus paying our debt.

Yet, interestingly, here, "Forgive us our debts…" is not a prayer for salvation. The context assumes those praying in this way already know God as their Father.

Jesus taught that we could approach our Father, appealing to Him to "forgive us our debts." But, Romans 8:1 tells us that those who are in Christ have no condemnation. So, to what is Jesus referring to when He speaks of debt?

Two details clue us in. First, in Matthew 6:14, Jesus says, "For if you forgive others their offenses…" This is where translators find the concept of trespasses, relating to verse twelve. And in Luke's version of the model prayer, he writes, "Forgive us our sins…" (Luke 11:4). These references provide us the first sign that Jesus is giving an example of praying for forgiveness of sins.

Secondly, this verse shows us that just like we have debts (or trespasses), we also have those who are our debtors (or those who trespass against us). In context, this does not refer to a great spiritual debt that someone owes us, but rather speaks to the forgiveness that should occur because the relationship is not as it should be.

This prayer encourages those who have a relationship with God to come to Him daily in repentance and confession of sin. Followers of Jesus will continually go to God in repentance, asking for forgiveness when they disobey because they now see their sin as God does.

> FOLLOWERS OF JESUS WILL CONTINUALLY GO TO GOD IN REPENTANCE, ASKING FOR FORGIVENESS WHEN THEY DISOBEY BECAUSE THEY NOW SEE THEIR SIN AS GOD DOES.

"But wait!" you say. "Since the Bible teaches that those who are reconciled to God through Christ have no condemnation, why would we need to ask for forgiveness continually if we are already justified?"

Let me illustrate: Imagine a couple, Jack and Diane. They have been married for a few months and have a massive argument because Jack has done something dumb (isn't that how it always happens, guys?).

While at work, Jack begins thinking about what he's done and how he was out of line. Talking to a few of his coworkers, he informs them of his plan to apologize to Diane when he gets off work.

They respond with ridicule, "You don't need to do that! What you did wasn't that bad. She isn't going to leave you. After all, we were at your wedding, and she said she'd be faithful to you for better or for worse. This is just the worse part, so she'll get over it!"

Confused, and rightly so, Jack looks at the group and replies, "You're right, she isn't going to leave me. But I also promised to love and be faithful in our relationship. I need to uphold my side of the covenant."

Friends, this is precisely the reason we are to react in repentance toward God when we sin.

If we say, "We have no sin," we are deceiving ourselves, and the truth is not in us. If we confess our sins, he is faithful and righteous to forgive us our sins and to cleanse us from all unrighteousness. If we say, "We have not sinned," we make him a liar, and his word is not in us.
(1 John 1:8-10)

Later in Matthew, the gospel writer recounts the time Jesus told a parable showing God's willingness to forgive.

For this reason, the kingdom of heaven can be compared to a king who wanted to settle accounts with his servants. When he began to settle accounts, one who owed ten thousand talents was brought before him. Since he did not have the money to pay it back, his master commanded that he, his wife, his children, and everything he had be sold to pay the debt.

At this, the servant fell facedown before him and said, "Be patient with me, and I will pay you everything." Then the master of that servant had compassion, released him, and forgave him the loan. (Matthew 18:23-27)

Through sincere confession and repentance, we make our side of the covenant right, and God mercifully forgives!

THOSE WHO SEEK FORGIVENESS FROM GOD MUST ALSO FORGIVE OTHERS

God is able and willing to forgive! However (and this is a BIG however), there is a caveat to this forgiveness. Those who seek forgiveness from God must also forgive others.

Let's continue the parable from Matthew 28. The servant was forgiven and now we see his response.

*That servant went out and found one of his fellow
servants who owed him a hundred denarii. He grabbed
him, started choking him, and said, "Pay what you
owe!"*

*At this, his fellow servant fell down and began begging
him, "Be patient with me, and I will pay you
back." But he wasn't willing. Instead, he went and
threw him into prison until he could pay what was
owed. When the other servants saw what had taken
place, they were deeply distressed and went and
reported to their master everything that had
happened. Then, after he had summoned him, his
master said to him, "You wicked servant! I forgave
you all that debt because you begged me. Shouldn't you
also have had mercy on your fellow servant, as I had
mercy on you?" And because he was angry, his master
handed him over to the jailers to be tortured until he
could pay everything that was owed. So also my
heavenly Father will do to you unless every one of you
forgives his brother or sister from your heart.*
(Matthew 28:28-35)

For most, including myself, we have probably always understood, "And forgive us our debts, as we also have forgiven our debtors," to mean something like, "Forgive us and help us to forgive others," which, in one sense, it does mean. However, the word "as" is

46

a conjunction in Greek, which can also be interpreted as "like," "when," "how," or "just as."

Additionally, this verse is the only one in this prayer that receives clarification from Jesus. After the final verse of the model prayer, He adds:

For if you forgive others their offenses, your heavenly Father will forgive you as well. But if you don't forgive others, your Father will not forgive your offenses.
(Matthew 6:14-15)

Wait! Does this mean our salvation is contingent on our willingness to forgive? Not at all. We serve a perfect God, who is also perfect in forgiveness. He is able and even willing to forgive the sin of unforgiveness. But as we mature in our faith, we will grow in Christ-like forgiveness, ready and willing to forgive others as ("like," "when," "how," or "just as") our Father has forgiven us.

Forgiven people forgive people. If we expect to receive greater

> **FORGIVEN PEOPLE FORGIVE PEOPLE.**

forgiveness from God than we are willing to offer others, as those who were guilty of praying with meaningless words (Matt. 6:5-8), we are hypocrites.

"And forgive us our debts, as we also have forgiven our debtors," now becomes exceptionally weighty. It embraces two ideas that followers of Jesus must regularly pray:

- Father, forgive me and help me to forgive others.

and

- Father, forgive me in the same way I have forgiven others.

How would experiencing and offering this type of forgiveness impact your life— complete forgiveness of your sins against God, and complete forgiveness of others' sins against you?

Get on your knees and honestly and boldly declare to the Father today, "And forgive me my debts, as I also have forgiven my debtors." Then rise and forgive. Live to show the power of God's incredible forgiveness in your life.

QUESTIONS FOR CONSIDERATION

1. How have you been thinking wrongly of your sin? Is there a "pet" sin you've held on to that you need to let go?

2. Have you ever thought that something you've done isn't forgivable? How should God's willingness to forgive your sin change your view of forgiveness and His grace?

3. Who are you reluctant to forgive? How does viewing your situation through the parable of the unforgiving servant in Matthew 18 change your perspective?

– DELIVER US FROM EVIL –

And do not bring us into temptation, but deliver us from the evil one.
(Matthew 6:13)

Deeply studying this prayer opens our hearts and eyes to how we are to live as believers. God longs for us to walk in holiness. This truth becomes evident throughout these verses—"Our Father, Your name be honored as holy. Help me long for Your kingdom to come. Help me to live according to Your will. Help me to trust You. Forgive me as I obediently forgive others." What a high standard.

THIS PRAYER DOESN'T JUST REVEAL TO US GOD'S EXPECTATIONS; IT SHOWS US HOW TO ACCOMPLISH THEM.

But this prayer doesn't just reveal to us God's expectations; it shows us how to accomplish them.

Imagine not knowing how to swim and then one day deciding, on a whim, to jump in the deep end of the pool. You ask someone nearby what you should do as you prepare to jump, and she says, "Just swim." You respond, "Yes, I know, but how do I do that?" It becomes quickly apparent that knowing what to do is different than learning how to do it.

Christians should regularly pray to walk in holiness through God's strength, but how are we to do that?

AVOIDANCE OF EVIL

When Jesus prays, "and do not bring us into temptation," He is praying as one who experienced temptation. He understands what we are going through because He was tempted as we all are.

Then Jesus was led up by the Spirit into the wilderness to be tempted by the devil.
(Matthew 4:1)

For we do not have a high priest who is unable to sympathize with our weaknesses, but one who has been tempted in every way as we are, yet without sin.
(Hebrews 4:15)

Think for a moment about your spiritual shortcomings—those areas of which you're prone to give in to sin time and time again. It probably doesn't take but a second to come up with two or three areas to which you have difficulty resisting sin when tempted.

Jesus was tempted in all ways, like the rest of humanity, but there was a stark difference. Unlike us, Jesus is God, and He had no weaknesses. We, however, are prone to sin because there are many areas in which we are weak.

"KEEP TEMPTATION AWAY FROM ME"

Toward Jesus's final hours before His death, He was praying in the Garden of Gethsemane with Peter, James, and John. It was late in the night, and He left them in a specific area of the Garden while He went to pray on His own. After a bit, Jesus returned only to find them sleeping. He then gave them a challenge that reverberates to us in our weaknesses:

Then he came to the disciples and found them sleeping. He asked Peter, "So, couldn't you stay awake with me one hour? Stay awake and pray, so that you won't enter into temptation. The spirit is willing, but the flesh is weak."
(Matthew 26:40-41)

Isn't this exactly how you feel when you give in to temptation? You know in your spirit that you don't want to do it, but you just feel so weak. After you sin, you find yourself saying in your guilty feeling, "I'll never do that again," only to return repeatedly to that same point.

> **WE MUST PRAY ABOUT OUR WEAKNESSES BEFORE TEMPTATIONS COME.**

We must pray about our weaknesses before temptations come. Most of us don't think about tests, trials, and temptations before they hit us. But instead of solely being reactive to the situation, we should be proactive. Consider the difference it would make if you were to wake up every morning with your weaknesses in the front of your mind, praying for God to help you stand firm when temptations come.

In praying to avoid temptations, we are saying, "Father, keep temptation away from me." We must be on guard in our weaknesses, knowing the devil has plans to come against us daily, seeking to gain a foothold of sin in our lives.

Be sober-minded, be alert. Your adversary the devil is prowling around like a roaring lion, looking for anyone he can devour.
(1 Peter 5:8)

"KEEP ME AWAY FROM TEMPTATION"

Whether your weakness is lust, greed, anger, jealousy, gossip, or something else, you should be praying daily for God to keep those temptations away from you.

Yet, the reality we must confront is that we often find ourselves tempted, not because we have randomly stumbled upon it, but because we have pursued it. We wrongly believe we have the self-strength to balance on the high wire of temptation without falling.

The book of Proverbs warns of the dangers of temptation.

Can a man walk on burning coals
without scorching his feet?
(Proverbs 6:28)

A man walking on burning coals is sure to scorch his feet. In the same way, if you play with temptation, you will eventually fall prey to it.

> **IF YOU PLAY WITH TEMPTATION, YOU WILL EVENTUALLY FALL PREY TO IT.**

James offers the follower of Jesus sound doctrine on walking through these moments and making the decisions God would delight in.

Consider it a great joy, my brothers and sisters,
whenever you experience various trials, because you
know that the testing of your faith produces endurance.
(James 1:2-3)

What I find interesting about this passage is that the Greek word James uses for "trials" is the same word Jesus uses for "temptation" in Matthew 6:13. However, there is a contrasting difference. Jesus prays for God not to bring us to temptation, but James says that we can consider it joy when we face trials. Same word, different response.

The change in the outcome (keep it away/consider it joy) occurs from our spiritual response to the testing itself. We should prayerfully seek to bar ourselves from temptation (consideration of sinning) but celebrate with joy when we experience those moments as trials (meditating on godly wisdom and obedience). James gives clarity on how to make godly decisions so that times of testing may be joyful.

Now if any of you lacks wisdom, he should ask God—who gives to all generously and ungrudgingly— and it will be given to him.
(James 1:5)

We are to pray about our weaknesses before they come. We pray for temptations to stay away from us. But we also must pray to have the wisdom to avoid temptation.

When you act in godly wisdom, temptations to fall into sin can become trials to rise in obedience. And God promises to give His wisdom to those who seek it. If you want to live in godly obedience and stand

> **WHEN YOU ACT IN GODLY WISDOM, TEMPTATIONS TO FALL INTO SIN CAN BECOME TRIALS TO RISE IN OBEDIENCE.**

against temptation, you must ask for and then exercise this divine wisdom. Ask God, "How can I live with wisdom and purge these temptations from my life?"

No temptation has come upon you except what is common to humanity. But God is faithful; he will not allow you to be tempted beyond what you are able, but with the temptation he will also provide the way out so that you may be able to bear it.
(1 Corinthians 10:13)

God will provide you the wisdom and the way out of temptation. There may be some significant changes you have to implement to live by that wisdom, but know it will be worth it!

DELIVERANCE FROM EVIL

You may be reading this today and feel like there's absolutely nothing you can do to overcome your temptations. Sin has a stronghold on your life. You've fought it for years on your willpower, with nothing but defeat to show for it.

Remember, Jesus didn't just teach us to pray to avoid temptation, but He also prayed, "But deliver us from the evil one." You can be delivered from your sin today! Jesus wants to rescue you! In Romans 11, Jesus Himself is called the Deliverer.

> **YOU CAN BE DELIVERED FROM YOUR SIN TODAY! JESUS WANTS TO RESCUE YOU!**

And in this way all Israel will be saved, as it is written, The Deliverer will come from Zion; he will turn godlessness away from Jacob. And this will be my covenant with them when I take away their sins. (Romans 11:26-27)

Ask the Lord to deliver you from your sin. Confess them specifically to Him. We must treat our sins as God did—put them to death.

Are you ready to do battle with your sin? Heed the words of Charles Spurgeon,

What settings are you in when you fall? Avoid them. What props do you have that support your sin? Eliminate them. What people are you usually with? Avoid them. There are two equally damning lies Satan wants us to believe: 1) Just once won't hurt.

2) Now that you have ruined your life, you are beyond God's use, and might as well enjoy sinning. Learn to say no. It will be of more use to you than to be able to read Latin."
- Charles Spurgeon

QUESTIONS FOR CONSIDERATION

1. What temptation(s) has God helped you overcome in the recent past? How did it happen?

2. How does the forgiveness mentioned in Matthew 6:12 impact verse13?

3. Who in your life could you ask to help hold you accountable in your weaknesses?

– CONCLUSION –

For some of you reading this, perhaps this was your first time digging into this prayer. If you're like me, I was taught the Bible from childhood and had memorized this prayer at an early age, but I had not deeply considered many of these truths. As we wrap up our time together, I want to leave you with three significant challenges to take away from this study.

PRAYER SHOULD BE NATURAL, NOT HYPOCRITICAL

Whether you choose to recite this model prayer as a repetition to God or simply use it as a guide, remember that prayer should be natural and genuine. The whole reason Jesus was teaching on prayer in the first place was that it had become hypocritical rather than authentic. Christian, don't let your prayers become meaningless! Prayer is a beautiful gift and privilege given to us by our Father.

PRAYER SHOULD BE CONFORMAL, NOT TERRITORIAL

When we pray, we shouldn't defend and argue the things on our "wish list." When we pray, we are seeking to match our hearts and wills to God's. We discovered much of His heart through this model prayer.

Is it okay to pray for healing, our ideal outcomes of situations, and favor on our loved ones? Yes, of course. However, we must remember we are not God. He doesn't bow to us. We are to turn to Him, conforming our wills to His. We cry out, "God, even in my requests, may Your will be done, and may I faithfully submit to it."

PRAYER SHOULD BE RELATIONAL, NOT TRANSACTIONAL

This final overarching truth, in some ways, combines the previous two. Do your prayers look more like a business transaction than a conversation? God is not your spiritual genie. He is not your bank teller. If you are in Christ, He is your Heavenly Father. You will find prayer much more rewarding and meaningful when you pursue a relationship with God rather than coming to Him with a list of demands.

Use your time and words to thank Him, adore Him, and open up to Him. When we embrace an attitude of praying without ceasing (1 Thess. 5:17), we will find ourselves drawing near to God and Him drawing near to us (James 4:8).

– APPENDIX 1 –
WHAT HAPPENED TO THE ENDING?

Many have noticed that when they study this prayer in a modern translation, it varies from the translation they may have read or memorized in the past. Compare the King James Version of this text to the Christian Standard Bible:

After this manner therefore pray ye: Our Father which art in heaven, Hallowed be thy name.
Thy kingdom come, Thy will be done in earth, as it is in heaven.
Give us this day our daily bread.
And forgive us our debts, as we forgive our debtors.
And lead us not into temptation, but deliver us from evil: For thine is the kingdom, and the power, and the

glory, for ever. Amen.
(Matthew 6:9-13, KJV)

Therefore, you should pray like this: Our Father in
heaven, your name be honored as holy.
Your kingdom come. Your will be done
on earth as it is in heaven.
Give us today our daily bread.
And forgive us our debts, as we also have forgiven our
debtors.
And do not bring us into temptation, but deliver us
from the evil one.
(Matthew 6:9-13, CSB)

The King James Version has an ending that feels very natural and conclusive. Without it, the prayer almost seems like it ends abruptly.

You probably noticed the Christian Standard Bible omits this ending, but it's not just this translation that does so. Practically every modern Bible translation does. Instead, they usually provide this ending in the footnote with a reference that says something like, "Some later manuscripts add, 'For yours is the kingdom and the power and the glory forever. Amen.'" What does this mean? Do the modern translators just decide to take this ending out for no reason?

First, let's discuss the translation process. Over 40 authors wrote the Bible in a span of about 1,500 years. All being inspired by God, they wrote in their native languages of Hebrew, Aramaic, and Greek. The passage we have focused on is in the New Testament, which was written in Greek.

Unlike today, where we can easily print multiple copies of documents, scribes painstakingly copied manuscripts by hand so the Bible could circulate. Today, we have found thousands of these ancient manuscript copies.

To help us understand the translating process, imagine for a moment that old children's game of "telephone." You remember it—a group of children sit in a line; someone whispers a message to the first child, and the child must whisper it to the person next to him. That person then whispers it to the next and so on. Then finally, the message is revealed by the last person in line. If the children were careful to communicate accurately, the final child would receive a very similar message to the one that began the game. If any of the children were not careful, the message would become highly inaccurate.

But let's pretend you didn't know the original message. If you wanted to determine it most accurately among the children, how would you do so? The obvious answer would be to ask the children who were sitting closest to the beginning of the line. The closer you are to the originator, the more accurate the message will be. Along with that, you could deduce the accuracy of the message if many children communicated the same message along the way, especially early on.

Now let's use this example to help us understand Bible translation. When translators begin their work, they seek to use the most accurate manuscripts as possible. Because the documents are hand-copied, translators will try to use the oldest manuscripts in conjunction with comparing those manuscripts with the other available copies, to determine their accuracy.

The King James Version, while still a good translation, was translated over 400 years ago. Since then, archeologists have discovered numerous more manuscripts than the translators had access to when translating the King James Version. As a result, they have concluded that this ending to the model prayer must have been added to the original writing somewhere along the way because it is not in the older manuscripts.[1]

Either way, if you want to pray this prayer and include the ending, feel free to do so. Jesus said to pray, "like this," so it's only to be used as a prayer guide anyway. There is much merit in proclaiming the kingdom, glory, and honor to be God's forever!

But remember, the goal of Bible translators is to bring us the most accurate version of God's Word in a language that we can understand. For this reason, this portion is not included in the main text anymore but is footnoted.

---

[1] For more information on the translation process, see the video, "Is the King James Version of the Bible the Most Accurate Translation?" at https://www.youtube.com/watch?v=FjfvtvmgT3s (Accessed Sept. 22, 2020).

– APPENDIX 2 –
MY FAVORITE BIBLE VERSES ON PRAYER

There are numerous verses in the Bible on prayer. For a quick reference, I have decided to include some of my favorites here for you. I encourage you to look up each of these verses and read them in context with their surrounding verses to correctly grasp their full meaning.

If I shut the sky so there is no rain, or if I command the grasshopper to consume the land, or if I send pestilence on my people, and my people, who bear my name, humble themselves, pray and seek my face, and turn from their evil ways, then I will hear from heaven, forgive their sin, and heal their land.
(2 Chronicles 7:13-14)

The LORD is near all who call out to him,
all who call out to him with integrity.
(Psalm 145:18)

The sacrifice of the wicked is detestable to the LORD,
but the prayer of the upright is his delight.
(Proverbs 15:8)

But I tell you, love your enemies and pray for those
who persecute you,
(Matthew 5:44)

If you remain in me and my words remain in you, ask
whatever you want and it will be done for you.
(John 15:7)

In the same way the Spirit also helps us in our
weakness, because we do not know what to pray for as
we should, but the Spirit himself intercedes for us with
inexpressible groanings.
(Romans 8:26)

Rejoice in hope; be patient in affliction; be persistent in
prayer.
(Romans 12:12)

*Don't worry about anything, but in everything,
through prayer and petition with thanksgiving, present
your requests to God.
(Philippians 4:6)*

*Rejoice always, pray constantly, give thanks in
everything; for this is God's will for you in Christ
Jesus.
(1 Thessalonians 5:16-18)*

*First of all, then, I urge that petitions, prayers,
intercessions, and thanksgivings be made for
everyone, for kings and all those who are in
authority, so that we may lead a tranquil and quiet
life in all godliness and dignity. This is good, and it
pleases God our Savior, who wants everyone to be
saved and to come to the knowledge of the truth.
(1 Timothy 2:1-4)*

*Is anyone among you suffering? He should pray. Is
anyone cheerful? He should sing praises.
(James 5:13)*

*Husbands, in the same way, live with your wives in an
understanding way, as with a weaker partner, showing
them honor as coheirs of the grace of life, so that your
prayers will not be hindered.
(1 Peter 3:7)*

This is the confidence we have before him: If we ask anything according to his will, he hears us. And if we know that he hears whatever we ask, we know that we have what we have asked of him.
(1 John 5:14-15)

– APPENDIX 3 –
HOW TO KNOW GOD AS YOUR FATHER

I don't want to assume that every person reading this book has come to know God in the way Jesus spoke of in Matthew 6. While it is true that we are all created in God's image, we are not all God's children.

Any time we disobey God and break His law, we sin. The sins we have committed have separated us from a holy God. The Bible tells us that everyone has sinned and, as a result, has fallen short of God's standard and is heading for eternal punishment in Hell (Romans 3:23, Romans 6:23).

However, God proved His love for us in that while we were still sinners, Christ died for us (Romans 5:8). Jesus lived the sinless life we couldn't live, being fully God and fully man, yet took our sins upon Himself when He died on the cross for us. Imagine a love so great that someone would be willing to die to pay a punishment you owe. That is the amazing love that Jesus has for you!

Three days later, Jesus rose from the dead, defeating death, sin, and the grave for those who are willing to repent of their sin and trust in Him alone for salvation.

Only those who are reconciled to God through Jesus's death and resurrection can know God as Father. The Bible tells us we must repent (or change our minds) about our sin and what we believe about Jesus (Acts 17:30), making Him Lord of our lives. Believing and confessing our faith in Jesus's death and resurrection and submitting to Him as Lord of our lives results in salvation and the beginning of knowing God as Father (Romans 10:9).

If you would like more information on how you can know God in this way, visit www.cometohim.org/salvation.

ABOUT THE AUTHOR

GJ Farmer is the founder of Come to Him Ministries and the Senior Pastor of Scottsville Baptist Church in Scottsville, KY. He holds degrees from Clear Creek Baptist Bible College (B.A.), Dallas Baptist University (M.A.), and New Orleans Baptist Theological Seminary (M.Div.), and is currently a doctoral student at Midwestern Baptist Theological Seminary. Most importantly, he is a husband to his wife, Hillary, and a father to his four children—Jack, Kenzie, Jocie, and Rhett. He enjoys spending time with his family, reading, and playing video games. For more information about GJ or Come to Him Ministries, visit www.cometohim.org.

C†H
COMETOHIM.ORG

Made in the USA
Monee, IL
08 August 2021

75225382R00052